UNLOCKING OUR UNDERSTANDING TO THE SEVEN SEALS OF REVELATION

By Douglas Cruz

AN APOCALYPTIC VIEW OF HUMANITY'S FUTURE REALITY

Copyright © 2014 by Douglas Cruz

Unlocking Our Understanding To The Seven Seals Of Revelation
An Apocalyptic View Of Humanity's Future Reality
by Douglas Cruz

Printed in the United States of America

ISBN 9781629523736

All rights reserved solely by the author. The author guarantees all contents are original and do not infringe upon the legal rights of any other person or work. No part of this book may be reproduced in any form without the permission of the author. The views expressed in this book are not necessarily those of the publisher.

Unless otherwise indicated, Bible quotations are taken from the King James Version.

www.xulonpress.com

This book is dedicated to
all of the saints of the last generation.

Table of Contents

Acknowledgment
ix
Foreword
xi
Introduction
xiii

Chapter 1   The Key That Unlocks Our Understanding of the Seven Seals ....Pg. 19

Chapter 2   The First Seal ....Pg. 25

Chapter 3   The Second Seal ....Pg. 31

Chapter 4   The Third Seal ....Pg. 35

Chapter 5   The Fourth Seal ....Pg. 41

Chapter 6   Revealing the Fifth Seal ....Pg. 49

Chapter 7   Revealing the Sixth Seal ....Pg. 67

Chapter 8   Revealing the Seventh Seal ....Pg. 81

Conclusion ....Pg. 85

Acknowledgment

Few books, if any, represent the work or thoughts of only one person. This one is no different. I am indebted to a great number of writers, historians, ministers, and friends from whom I have gleaned a great amount of information, material, and insight.

I would like to express my appreciation to the Xulon Press editorial committee and publishing staff for their contribution in making this book possible. I also thank Pastor Scott Bambrough for his encouragement and for giving me the opportunity to present this material in the form of a seminar at his congregation.

I am especially indebted to my wife, Debi, for her prayers, encouragement, and patience while I was writing this manuscript, and to my precious daughter, Melissa, who assisted me in preparing the power point presentation for my first eschatology seminar!

I thank also my sister, Anna Cruz, for taking out the time from her other duties for her invaluable contribution in assisting me during the shaping of this manuscript. To my good friend and brother, Chris Adams, a hearty thanks for uniquely designing the cover for this book. To another good friend, Reginaldo Duarte Jr. better known as "Reggie" for sharing his poem with us. Also, to my local congregation, with which I've shared much of this information throughout the years, I indeed express an attitude of gratitude for their prayers and encouragement.

Most of all, to the Holy Spirit who alone deserves the expression "Awesome" a great thank you for His Divine illumination in helping me to understand this apocalyptic vision. Without His inspiration this book would have never been produced.

Foreword

People are curious creatures as well as creatures of habit. What our future looks like is an ongoing question that fuels the mind as well as a sense of adventure. Why are we such curious creatures and what is so important about the future that such a vast amount of the Word of God is devoted to future events, future ramifications determined by present decision making and a future destination called eternity? Prophecy is contained throughout the Bible from Genesis to Revelation and has come in different mediums like: dreams, visions, divine revelation, the voice of God, and so forth.

God has given us all of this with the purpose of helping us to be sober, diligent, and prepared.

It is not just those living in the twenty-first century that are curious. Believe it or not Jesus' 12 disciples were also of the curious type; they had asked Jesus about the end times, yet instead of correcting their curiosity the Lord satisfied their curiosity in Matthew 24. Along with the vast number of people that are intrigued by the end times, there is also enough material that has been written on the subject that it can be hard for someone to decipher which book to read or which seminar to go to. As many books on the end times that there are, there is that many points of view—after all why write a book if you don't have new light to shed on the matter or something more to add to this subject in order to help us better understand such a difficult topic.

This book was written for that very reason, to help us better understand the future as given to us in Revelation and more specifically the seven seals. I have known the author for over 22 years, and the subject has been a passion of his for the majority of that time. He has spent much time studying, praying, and fasting over this subject these many years. The author has a great reverence for the Word of God and has taken considerable care to let the Word interpret the Word and not make it of private interpretation. The approach that the author has taken in explaining the end times is very effective in helping us make sense of this subject. His explanations put these events together through opening up the progression of the seven seals.

As a senior pastor for 20 years now, listening to the author share his heart on this subject, it has helped me to receive a better understanding of the end times and how it all works together. It has also helped open my eyes to the vast amount of connections that exist between Revelation's apocalyptic message and the Bible from beginning to end.

As you attempt to fill your curiosity of the future make it a habit of finding your answers in the Word of God.

By Bishop Scott Bambrough
Senior Pastor, Tucson Church of God of Prophecy

INTRODUCTION

Revelation is a fascinating and captivating book. It is the final book of the Bible, known as the apocalypse of end times or book of ultimate. In contrast, Genesis is known as the book of beginnings. In Genesis we find a river of foundational truths in seed form, which eventually flows throughout the scriptures to reach the sea of fulfillment, the book of Revelation. The writing of this book of Revelation is not only fascinating, but also very spiritual and mysterious. It is filled with certain figures of speech, such as types, symbols, numbers, and so forth, which have hidden meanings. However, by using proper biblical hermeneutic principles and the literal method of interpretation, one can discover the divine truths latent in this wonderful book.

Another important key that one must use to unlock and discover its meaning is to be in the Spirit. John the apostle tells us that he was in the Spirit, on the Lord's Day, when he received this apocalyptic vision. Unless one has been born again, that is, born of the Spirit, he or she will never be able to comprehend this spiritual book of Revelation. So if you haven't experience this new spiritual birth, I would encourage you to stop reading right now. Then get on your knees if possible, and ask God to forgive you of your sins, and invite Jesus Christ as Lord and Savior into your life: *"For he saith, I have heard thee in a time accepted, and in the day of salvation have I succored thee:*

behold, now is the accepted time; behold, now is the day of salvation" (2 Corinthians 6:2).

We must first of all understand and agree that God is the spiritual author of these sacred scriptures. John received this vision through divine revelation and inspiration. It was the Holy Spirit, through an angel, who revealed to John the prophetic events that he saw. It is just as vital that we too be filled with this same Spirit, in order to understand and receive illumination of this end-time vision. Moreover, the book of *Daniel*, which is a companion book found in the Old Testament, will also be referred to along with the book of *Revelation*. For Daniel was given a similar vision that included certain details which help clarify John's vision. However, the prophet Daniel was told by Gabriel (the archangel), to seal up the words of his vision. We, the Church of the last days and end-time chosen generation of believers, can count ourselves blessed in knowing that God has reserved the unveiling of these truths for our day.

The book of Revelation was primarily written for the Church of the end time or last days. Though natural Israel is implicitly mentioned and dealt with throughout this book, especially in the latter half of the approximately seven-year period, the main focus will still be with the new spiritual Israel (the Jewish and Gentile Church; *Galatians 6:16*).

John, the beloved apostle, was told by Christ, in the very first chapter to write down in a book the events that he had seen and to send it to the seven churches that were located in Asia Minor (*Revelation 1:11,19*). Furthermore, as we reach the conclusion of this book, we see Jesus once again telling John to testify about these things in the churches (*Revelation 22:16*). The question we must ask ourselves now is; "Why should John testify to the Church all these events, if she was not going to be here on earth to experience them as some erroneously believe and teach?" The truth of the matter is that the Church of the last days will be here to accomplish and fulfill God's purposes, until

INTRODUCTION

she is taken (raptured) prior to the outpouring of the fullness of God's wrath.

Let us now proceed with the subject at hand: *Unlocking Our Understanding to the Seven Seals of Revelation*. The Seven Seals are basically an introduction or synopsis of the entire events that are going to occur toward the end of this age. By reading carefully these Seven Seals that are mostly found in chapter six, one should be able to get a quick glimpse of future events.

Another interesting fact that you will notice as you read this book is that God many times uses numbers to illustrate or represent persons, creatures, things, or events of great importance. We find one such outstanding number to be the number seven. The significance of this number, according to scripture, means perfection and completeness. This number seven can either represent perfect goodness, or it can be represented in a perfect negative sense. It is a number that is frequently used not only concurrent within the Seven Seals, but throughout the book of Revelation.

Please observe the following list of examples found in this particular book that use the number *seven*; the seven churches [*Revelation 1:4*]; the seven Spirits [*Revelation 1:4*] the seven stars and seven golden candlesticks [*Revelation 1:20*]; the seven lamps [*Revelation 4:5*]; the Seven Seals [*Revelation 5:1*]; the seven angels [*Revelation 8:6*]; the seven trumpets [*Revelation 8:6*]; the seven thunders [*Revelation 10:4*]; the seven last plagues which are the seven golden vials full of the wrath of God [*Revelation 15:1, 6-8*]; the seven heads and seven mountains [*Revelation 17:9-11*].

Another number of great importance, that we should concern ourselves with is the number three-and-a-half years; the scriptures express the number in this manner, time, times, and a half time. The last seven-year period of mankind's rule on earth will be divided into two segments of three-and-a-half years each. The first three-and-a-half year period will be a time for the Church to accomplish the purposes of God by paralleling the ministry of her Head, Jesus Christ *(Ephesians 4:11-13)*. The ministry of Christ on earth lasted three-and-a-half years; therefore the Church will have a similar three-and-a-half year ministry and purpose.

These purposes will include the unification of all true sheep (Jew and Gentile believers) into the one Body of Christ *(John 10:16; 17:23)*; the reaping of the harvest *(Matthew 13:39)*; by fulfilling the great commission *(Matthew 28:18-20)*; and Her perfection and final deliverance *(Ephesians 5:26, 27)*.

The other three-and-a-half year segment or period will be a time characterized by the complete reign of Satan through his beastly masterpiece, the Antichrist *(Revelation 13:5)*. God will also continue or resume, during this same time, to deal specifically with the children of Israel *(Revelation 12:13-17)*. His dealings will be through the ministries of the two witnesses-prophets *(Revelation 11:3-13)*.

Furthermore, I would like to share a word of advice! All who endeavor to understand and interpret these seven seals will definitely need to maintain a prayerful attitude and dependence upon the guiding illumination of the Holy Spirit. Please read how the disciple's understanding was unlocked in *Luke 24:45*.

Finally, remember the first rule of hermeneutics, "Scripture interprets scripture," which must be applied to this prophetic vision. The Holy Spirit used men to write scripture. Then He used their scripture to write more scripture, therefore we should use scripture to interpret scripture. The Bible is its own best commentary! As God is the author of scripture, we must totally rely on Him to help us interpret and rightly divide these Seven Seals. Otherwise misinterpretation, misapplication, and confusion will be the result of our exposition.

This expositor has diligently tried to minimize his comments concerning certain details, in explaining these eschatological events and have rather allowed the scriptures to speak for themselves. But in certain instances, I felt the need to elaborate extensively on some of the events, for clarification purposes. Moreover, I have carefully written this book in light of the precaution given to us in Revelation *22:18, 19: " For I testify unto every man that heareth the words of the prophecy of this book, If any man shall add unto these things, God shall add unto him the plagues that are written in this book:*

And if any man shall take away from the words of the book of this prophecy, God shall take away his part out of the book of life, and out of the holy city, and from the things which are written in this book."

Only time will tell whether this exposition is in line with God's timetable of events or whether I missed the mark. The King James Version (1611) will be used in quoting text in this book.

Chapter 1

The Key That Unlocks Our Understanding of the Seven Seals

The book of *Revelation* was written in chronological order. We all agree that the sequence of events follow their God-ordained course. One set of events follow another set of events. The problem I discovered with my early reading and study of this book, as with reading the writings (books, articles) of other expositors, was the following: while one begins to read the first five chapters of this book, everything seems to run smooth. But when one reaches chapter six and begins to read about most of the Seven Seals contained in this chapter, one makes the mistake in assuming that these seals represent the first set of judgments. Then as one continues to read the other chapters, the logical assumption is made that following the Judgment of the Seals, other sets will follow; such sets as the Judgment of the Seven Trumpets, succeeded by the Seven Thunders and finally the Seven last Plagues.

To my surprise though, God in a very gracious manner, enabled me to slip from this erroneous assumption by revealing to me the key that unlocked my understanding to the Seven Seals and the rest of the book of *Revelation*. The simple but mysterious key is that the Seven Seals, as I mentioned in my introduction, are a synopsis or a brief condensed outline of all the events that are mentioned in the other chapters of *Revelation*. The key or secret is to know which events that are recorded for us in the books of *Daniel, Revelation,* and other books of the *canon*, can be placed under each Seal. You see, each particular Seal represent certain brief events that are more fully elaborated and explained in detail, in the other chapters of *Revelation*, with the exception of the first Seal. Most of the details of this Seal are given to us by the prophet Daniel in his book.

As a result of much praying and fasting, God, by His Spirit, has illuminated my understanding on how to unlock and place, under each Seal, the following events and judgments recorded in Revelation. One quick example of what I am talking about is to look at Seal number six. The passage for this particular Seal can be found in chapter 6, verses 12-17. But let us pay close attention to verse 14: *"And the heaven departed as a scroll when it is rolled together; and every mountain and island were moved out of their places."* This Seal represents the judgment of the seven last Plagues recorded for us in chapters 16 through 19. As one reads *Revelations 16:17-21,* you will discover, in graphic details, why the mountains and islands are moved out of their place as a result of this last seventh plague (great earthquake). But before we begin to unlock the Seven Seals that are explained in the subsequent chapters of this book, let us now look at a special Seal that God has reserved for us.

According to *Revelation, chapter seven*, John declares to us that before God begins to pour out His judgments upon the earth, sea, and humanity, He is going to send the angels to seal His servants with a special seal of protection. All who are espoused to Christ during this time will be sealed. These servants will have to belong to the true bride of Christ, His Church and New Covenant community, made up of both Jews and Gentiles (*1 Corinthians 12:13)*, to be included in this number. John was able to count the number of Jewish servants which amounted to 144,000; but when he attempted to count the number of Gentile servants, the amount was too large for him to count. *Revelation 7:9 "After this I beheld, and, lo, a great multitude, which no man could number, of all nations, and kindreds, and people, and tongues, stood before the throne, and before the Lamb, clothed with white robes, and palms in their hands."* The Church of God, like I mentioned in my introduction, will still be here to accomplish and fulfill her God-given purpose, until she is raptured from this period of tribulation.

Chapter 2

THE FIRST SEAL

Revealing the Rider on the White Horse

Revelation 6:2
"And I saw, and behold a white horse: and he that sat on him had a bow; and a crown was given unto him: and he went forth conquering, and to conquer."

The rider of this white horse is going to be an extraordinary individual. One expositor that I read went as far as to say that this rider represented our Lord Jesus Christ. To this commentary I must disagree! This rider is seen wearing a crown, handling a bow, and conquering. But on the contrary, when Christ returns the second time to conquer His enemies and establish His Kingdom, we obviously see Him wearing many crowns and handling a rod of iron according to *Revelation 19:11-16*.

Further, this first rider, with the other riders that follow, are symbolically four apocalyptic sinister riders and their horses that will literary bring deception, destruction, and death to one-fourth of the human race. There is absolutely nothing benevolent about this rider, though he rides a seemingly benevolent white horse. Who then is this rider upon this white horse?

The rider on the white horse represents a super-intelligent, political, religious, and military leader who will, in his diplomatic dealings, use his political-religious influence to conquer, by deception, the minds and hearts of many people; please read *Daniel 11:21-31; 2 Corinthians 11:13-15*. This individual will present himself to Israel as their long-awaited Messiah. He will then make a peace treaty or covenant of peace with Israel for a period not lasting more than seven years. This alliance of peace will then be broken and stopped by him, sometime during the midst of this period: *Daniel 9:26, 27; Matthew 24:15*.

This rider will be in control of a global governmental system. The Satanic and beastly nature of this rider's modern Babylonian system called the New World Order is clearly described in the Bible prophecies of the end times. Here is a brief list of this individual's evil behavior and practice that will continue or last for approximately seven years, but especially the final three-and-a-half years of this period: (*Daniel 8:13, 14*) 2,300 days = a period of 6 years, 3 months and 3 weeks.

1) The Rider-Antichrist will be a fierce and cruel dictator; *"A king of fierce countenance shall arise in the latter time" Daniel 8:23*

2) The Rider-Antichrist will deceptively gain his authority with a small group as described in *Daniel 11:23 "And after the league made with him he shall work deceitfully: for he shall come up, and shall become strong with a small people."*

3) The Rider-Antichrist will come to world power as a man of peace; *"And in his estate shall stand up a vile person, to whom they shall not give the honor of the kingdom: but he shall come in peaceably, and obtain the kingdom by flatteries; He shall enter peaceably even upon the fattest places of the province ..." Daniel 11:21, 24a*

4) The Rider-Antichrist's global economic policy will cause many to prosper *"And through his policy also he shall cause craft to prosper in his hand;"* Daniel 8:25a

5) The Rider-Antichrist will use his political power to change times and laws; *"And he shall speak great words against the most High, and shall wear out the saints of the most High,* and think to change times and laws: *and they shall be given into his hand until a time and times and dividing of time (*three-and-a-half years*)."* Daniel *7:25* (emphasis mine). The abnormal, perverse, bizarre, and weird will be the normal standard in that day.

6) The Rider-Antichrist will declare war on the saints; Daniel 7:25a; 8:12, 24; Revelation 13:7 *"And it was given unto him to make war with the saints and to overcome them: and power was given him over all kindreds, and tongues, and nations."*

7) The Rider-Antichrist will have a strong military force; *"And with the arms of a flood shall they be overflown from before him, and shall be broken." "And arms shall stand on his part."* Daniel 11:22, 31

8) The Rider-Antichrist will probably be a homosexual; *"Neither shall he regard the God of his fathers, nor the desire of women, nor regard any god: for he shall magnify himself above all"* Daniel 1:37. The reason I say this is because the Devil operates by a principle of reversal. Anything normal and decent that God has created, he perverts and does the opposite. And since the body of this individual will eventually be possessed by the Devil (*Revelation 13:2)* he will manifest or should I say devil-fest his perverted lifestyle, through him.

9) The Rider-Antichrist, with the diabolical support of the false prophet, will force everyone to make their allegiance, by taking the mark of the beast; (*Revelation 13:16-18*).

10) The whole world will worship this beast (Antichrist) who will be the personification of humanism, narcissism and all of the other evil ideologies combined; *"And he shall magnify himself in his heart, and by peace shall destroy many"; "And the king shall do according to his will; and magnify himself above every god, and shall speak marvelous things against the God of gods, and shall prosper till the indignation be accomplished: for that that is determined shall be done." Daniel 8:25b;11:36 "And all that dwell upon the earth shall worship him, whose names are not written in the book of life of the lamb slain from the foundation of the world." Revelation 13:8*

Chapter 3

THE SECOND SEAL

Revealing the Rider of the Red Horse

Revelation 6:3, 4
"And when he had opened the second seal, I heard the second beast say, Come and see. And there went out another horse that was red: and power was given to him that sat thereon to take peace from the earth, and that they should kill one another: and there was given unto him a great sword."

The Rider of the Red Horse represents massive bloodshed as the result of global homicides (all types of killings), which will eventually lead to a massive war. The peaceful security that nations and people groups have safely trusted in throughout the years, will soon be a thing of the past. The hedge of protection that has been upon humanity will be abruptly interrupted by the rider of this apocalyptic red horse. Get your house in order, my friend, for some extraordinary home protection, because when this rider arrives, he will radically change the way you live in society.

He will instigate worldwide violence and international terrorism in the form of war, race riots, ethnic cleansing (genocide), increase of suicides and suicide bombings, homicides by organized crime against humanity, friction between political and religious factions, urban and suburban gang killings, violent mass protest against the disparity between the rich and poor, social injustice, murders resulting from broken marriages and dysfunctional families. Deadly chemical, biological, and nuclear accidents will cause widespread pandemics, which will lead to hundreds and perhaps thousands of deaths. The breakdown of our society as we know it will become our daily reality.

It is under this Second Seal that I felt led to begin placing the trumpet judgments. The details for this particular seal are given to us in the six trumpet judgments recorded for us in *Revelation 9:13-19*. By reading this passage of scripture one can clearly see that one third of men or mankind will be destroyed, as a result of this warfare. It's quite possible that smaller wars and internal conflicts may occur simultaneously while the other trumpet judgments are happening, culminating into this six trumpet judgment (major warfare). Our blessed Lord and Savior, Jesus Christ, and Paul, the apostle, provide us with certain details, in their predictions, about this chaotic and dangerous time we will face.

I. The prediction of Christ concerning this time;
   A) *"And ye shall hear of wars and rumors of wars: see that ye be not troubled: for all these things must come to pass, but the end is not yet. For nation shall rise against nation, and kingdom against kingdom: and there shall be famines, and pestilences, and earthquakes, in divers places." "And because iniquity shall abound, the love of many shall wax cold." "But as the days of Noah were, so shall also the coming of the Son of man be. For as in the days that were before the flood they were eating and drinking, marrying and giving in marriage, until the day that Noah entered into the ark, And knew not until the flood came, and took them all*

away; so shall also the coming of the Son of man be." Matthew 24:6, 7, 12, 37-39

B) *"But when ye shall hear of wars and commotions, be not terrified: for these things must first come to pass; but the end is not by and by. Then said he unto them, Nation shall rise against nation, and kingdom against kingdom:" Luke 21:9, 10*

II. The prediction of Paul concerning this time;
"But of the times and the seasons, brethren, ye have no need that I write unto you. For yourselves know perfectly that the day of the Lord so cometh as a thief in the night. For when they shall say, **Peace** and **safety**; *then sudden destruction cometh upon them, as travail upon a woman with child; and they shall not escape.*

But ye, brethren, are not in darkness, that that day should overtake you as a thief. Ye are all the children of light, and the children of the day: we are not of the night, nor of darkness. Therefore let us not sleep, as do others; but let us watch *and be sober. For they that* sleep *sleep in the night; and they that be drunken are drunken in the night. But let us, who are of the day, be sober, putting on the breastplate of faith and love; and for a helmet, the hope of salvation. For God hath not appointed us to wrath, but to obtain salvation by our Lord Jesus Christ,"*

1 Thessalonians 5:1-8 (emphasis is mine)

Chapter 4

THE THIRD SEAL

Revealing the Rider of the Black Horse

Revelation 6:5, 6
"And when he had opened the third seal, I heard the third beast say, Come and see. And I beheld, and lo a black horse; and he that sat on him had a pair of balances in his hand. And I heard a voice in the midst of the four beasts say, a measure of wheat for a penny, and three measures of barley for a penny; and see thou hurt not the oil and the wine."

This black horse and its rider represent a terrible famine that will affect one-third of our natural resources, which eventually will affect one-third of the world's population. But before this famine begins, notice the last clause in verse six which states: *"...and see thou hurt not the oil and the wine."* One must ask the question, why did one of the seraphims tell the rider of this horse, not to hurt the oil and the wine? One possible answer to this question is that God, who is rich in mercy, may allow the nations of the world, that are heavily dependent and addicted to this oil (petroleum), to continue running the machinery, that operates their cities and countries. God will even allow these nations to continue their times of festivities and social events, by sparing the wine and vineyard industries.

A more important reason, I think, the fresh wine (not fermented grape juice) is especially spared, will be for the saints to continue its use in their celebration of the Lord's Supper. Praise God! This New Testament ordinance that was instituted by Christ encourages the saints to remember and appreciate their Savior's sacrificial death, until He returns again. And in a personal note, this poor minister of the gospel can truly appreciate a fresh cold glass of grape juice anytime. Not only is this grape juice drink delicious, but it is more beneficial with antioxidants than my favorite Caribbean beverage called Malta.

The details of this Seal are recorded and expressed through the following three trumpet judgments, which I will place under this particular seal. Please understand that these three trumpet judgments are primarily directed toward the sinful inhabitants and nations of this world. God, who is rich in mercy, is not willing that any should perish, but that all should acknowledge their sinful condition and repent (*2 Peter 3:9*).

There is a twofold purpose for these trumpet judgments. First, God will use them to finally shake and awaken the nations to the reality that the end of this age is approaching (*Hebrews 12:26, 27*), and second, to alert and mightily anoint the Church with the power of His Holy Spirit, as promised in the symbol of the latter rain (*James 5:8, 9*). This spiritual power will enable her to effectively proclaim the gospel of Christ's kingdom, to a lost and dying world. The Church must understand that these trumpet judgments will prepare the nations of the world to hear the wonderful message of redemption that she will bring to them through her final evangelistic and missionary efforts.

There is a reason why the Church of God must endure these first trumpet judgments along with the rest of the world. Jesus prayed in the garden of Gethsemane, for His Father not to take the Church out of the world, but for Him to keep them from the evil; please read *John 17:15* and also *Revelation 3:10*.

We have an Old Testament account of how God kept and allowed the Children of Israel, while they were in captivity in the land of Egypt (a type of the world), to endure, along with the Egyptians, the first three plagues of judgment. They endured, until God placed a hedge of protection over them from the remaining plagues; *"And I will sever in that day the land of Goshen, in which my people dwell, that no swarms of flies shall be there; to the end thou mayest know that I am the Lord in the midst of the earth" Exodus 8:22.* Now let's look at this third Seal that will destroy one-third of our natural resources and population, as expressed in the following three trumpets:

FIRST TRUMPET JUDGMENT—*Revelation 8:7 "The first angel sounded, and there followed hail and fire mingled with blood, and they were cast upon the earth: and the third part of trees was burnt up, and all green grass was burnt up."*

Obviously this judgment will affect one third of the world's agricultural food supply; which means great hunger for the masses. Jesus' prediction found in *Matthew 24:7b* confirms this when He stated, *"...and there shall be famines."* Many people will die of starvation, as the world's food supplies dwindles. Many stores, supermarkets, restaurants, fast and slow food places will probably go out of business, as a result of this tragedy. Our chicken and steak platters will only be a memory for some of us. This indeed will be a devastating judgment for believers to see as a *first sign* that we have now entered the beginning of the trumpet judgments.

SECOND TRUMPET JUDGMENT—*Revelation 8:8, 9 "And the second angel sounded, and as it were a great mountain burning with fire was cast into the sea: and the third part of the sea became blood; And the third part of the creatures which were in the sea, and had life, died; and the third part of the ships were destroyed."*

As we look into this judgment, we notice that this great mountain burning with fire is probably symbolically portraying part of an asteroid falling with great heat into the ocean and causing it to boil, thereby destroying one-third of its sea creatures. Again, what does this mean for the inhabitants of the earth? It means that one-third of the world's seafood supply will perish, thus making the seafood industry extremely rare and expensive for the average man or woman to purchase. This tragedy will also contribute to the world's hunger pains. You brethren can forget about your seafood platters; that dish will also be a thing of the past.

THIRD TRUMPET JUDGMENT—*Revelation 8:10, 11 "And the third angel sounded, and there fell a great star from heaven, burning as it were a lamp, and it fell upon the third part of the rivers, and upon the fountains of waters; And the name of the star is called Wormwood: and the third part of the waters became wormwood; and many men died of the waters, because they were made bitter."*

This third judgment, which symbolically portrays a meteorite, will affect one third of the world's fresh water supply by making them too deadly to drink. Many people will eventually die of thirst. There is absolutely no other liquid on earth that can satisfy a person's thirst like a fresh, cold glass of water. We can stock up now on fresh bottled water, but eventually this vital resource will also diminish and become too expensive for the average man or woman to purchase in small or large quantities. The limited fresh water supply will be rationed out to its citizens by the New World Order Government that will be implemented to control the remaining world population.

The Church will have to mature in her faith before this happens, in order to survive this famine of hunger and thirst, by trusting in the promises of God to supply her needs. One such promise is, *"But my God shall supply all your need according to his riches in glory by Christ Jesus" Philippians 4:19.* Our

God is well able to supply the necessary food and water we will need to survive, but not in the abundance that we have been accustomed to. There will be days when we will experience some hunger and some thirst; but please don't give up and become despondent! Just continue to trust in His promises, for our God is a faithful God. Amen!

A scene from John's vision, about this tragic event, can be a source of consolation for some of us, as we patiently suffer, along with the world, this particular judgment. He writes that after we have been delivered from these days of tribulation, God will minister and comfort us; *"And I said unto him, Sir, thou knowest. And he said to me, these are they which came out of great tribulation, and have washed their robes, and made them white in the blood of the Lamb. Therefore are they before the throne of God, and serve him day and night in his temple: and he that sitteth on the throne shall dwell among them.* They shall hunger no more, neither thirst any more; *neither shall the sun light on them, nor any heat. For the Lamb which is in the midst of the throne shall feed them, and shall lead them unto living* fountains *of waters: and God shall wipe away all tears from their eyes." Revelation 7:14-17* (emphasis is mine).

Chapter 5

THE FOURTH SEAL

Revealing the Rider of the Pale Horse

Revelation 6:7, 8
"And when he had opened the fourth seal, I heard the voice of the fourth beast say, Come and see. And I looked, and behold a pale horse: and his name that sat on him was Death, and Hell followed with him. And power was given unto them over the fourth part of the earth, to kill with sword, and with hunger, and with death, and with the beasts of the earth."

This Pale Horse and its Rider represents the inescapable reality of Death and Hell. This fourth seal is the final outcome and result of the previous two Seals (represented by the three trumpet judgments), plus the fourth, fifth, and six trumpet judgments which I will expound on in a moment. Nevertheless, the sad reality is that one-fourth of the unrepentant human race will perish. Presently, the world's population is getting close to eight billion people. So we are looking at about two billion inhabitants being wiped out from this planet as a result of these judgments. Now let's look at these three remaining trumpet judgments that are part of this seal:

THE FOURTH TRUMPET JUDGMENT — *Revelation 8:12, 13 "And the fourth angel sounded, and the third part of the sun was smitten, and the third part of the moon, and the third part of the stars; so as the third part of them was darkened, and the day shone not for a third part of it, and the night likewise."*

God is going to sharply strike at these three celestial objects (the sun, moon, and stars). The blow will be so devastating that it will prevent these heavenly bodies to shine forth about a third of the day and a third of the night. What does this judgment mean and how will it affect us and the world? In general, our minds and bodies are accustomed to a 24-hour day. We usually work for eight hours, have leisure for another eight hours and finally sleep for the remaining eight. But this particular judgment will reduce or shorten our normal 24-hour day, to a 16-hour day, by removing eight hours (a third).

The discomfort that our minds and bodies will feel will be worse than jet-lag. People who have flown by jet through different time zones can relate to this miserable condition to a certain degree. When one should be wide awake and ready to face the day, the body wants to rest and sleep. The opposite can be just as disturbing. When the body should be resting and asleep, it finds itself wide awake. These short days and nights will disrupt everyone's daily routine and lifestyle, not only here in the States, but also on a worldwide scale.

Another reason for this judgment, which in a sense is a disguised blessing for the believer, is the promise Christ made to His disciples. Jesus stated in *Matthew 24:22, "And except those days should be shortened, there should no flesh be saved: but for the elect's sake those days shall be shortened."* Thank God that these days of tribulation are going to be shortened, not for the sake of the wicked, but for the sake of the righteous. Hallelujah!

He also stated in *Luke 21:25, 26; "And there shall be signs in the sun, and in the moon, and in the stars; and upon the earth distress of nations, with perplexity; the sea and the waves roaring; Men's hearts failing them for fear, and for looking after those things which are coming on the earth: for the powers of heaven shall be shaken."* When this judgment occurs, mankind will be forced, once again, to acknowledge the awesome power of God!

THE FIFTH TRUMPET JUDGMENT — *Revelation 9:1-11*
"And the fifth angel sounded, and I saw a star fall from heaven unto the earth: and to him was given the key of the bottomless pit. And he opened the bottomless pit; and there arose a smoke out of the pit, as the smoke of a great furnace; *and the sun and the air were darkened by reason of the smoke of the pit. And there came out of the smoke locusts upon the earth: and unto them was given* power, *as the scorpions of the earth have power. And it was commanded them that they should not hurt the grass of the earth, neither any green thing, neither any tree; but only those men which have not the seal of God in their foreheads. And to them it was given that they should not kill them, but that they should be tormented five months: and their torment was as the torment of a scorpion, when he striketh a man. And in those days shall men seek death, and shall not find it; and shall desire to die, and death shall flee from them. And the shapes of the locusts were like unto horses prepared unto battle; and on their heads were as it were crowns like gold, and their faces were as the faces of men. And they had hair as the hair of women, and their teeth were as the teeth of lions. And they had breastplates, as it were breastplates of iron; and the sound of their wings was as the sound of chariots of many horses running to battle. And they had tails like unto scorpions, and there were stings in their tails: and their power was to hurt men five months. And they had a king over them, which is the angel of the bottomless pit, whose name in the Hebrew tongue is Abaddon, but in the Greek tongue hath his name Apollyon."*

This judgment is going to be the horror of horrors. When one reads this passage of scripture, it sounds like one is reading a script for some science fiction horror movie. Believe me that this is not another phony horror movie, but a soon coming horrific reality. An angel from heaven will come down and release these heinous creatures from the bottomless pit. They will ascend and attack mankind with a vicious vengeance, for approximately five months.

Now, in order for us to understand who these creatures are and why they are so vindictive, one will have to return to the historical first book of Genesis. There is a theory, which quite possibly might be true, found in *(Genesis 6:1-9)*, of an evil deed that some of the sons of God committed. The term, sons of God, are taught by many theological seminaries to be the descendants from the godly line of Seth, Adam and Eve's third son. But a closer look shows this term is also used, in the passages found in *Job 1:6; 2:1; 38:7*, to describe the angelic host of heaven.

With this view in mind, it's quite possible that some of the angels that fell with Satan *(Revelation 12:4)*, were allowed to cross a dimension from the spirit world ("left their habitation" *Jude 1:5, 6*) to the natural world, by transforming themselves into human males. Then they, through their evil lust, were able to copulate with the beautiful, but evil women of the earth. What was their main purpose and motive for doing this? It was to contaminate the genetic pool of the human race. This they did, in hopes of preventing the Messianic promise of redemption, given to Adam and Eve, found in *(Genesis 3:15)*; from being fulfilled.

What resulted though from these illicit sexual encounters of another kind, were the birth of literal giants. These giants of huge stature caused the earth to be filled with violence and corruption through their evil deeds. God had to eventually destroy the known world back then, through the flood (deluge), but judged and cast into the bottomless pit, these fallen angels who had committed this great evil (*2 Peter 2:4, 5*). Thus, when these fallen angels are finally released from their chain of darkness, they will not reappear as human males, but rather as locust-looking monsters, from the bottomless pit.

THE SIX TRUMPET JUDGMENT—*Revelation 9:13-21*
"And the sixth angel sounded, and I heard a voice from the four horns of the golden altar which is before God, Saying to the sixth angel which had the trumpet, Loose the four angels which are bound in the great river Euphrates. And the four angels were loosed, which were prepared for an hour, and a day, and a month, and a year, for to slay the third part of men. And the number *of the army of the horsemen were two hundred thousand: and I heard the number of them. And thus I saw the horses in the vision, and them that sat on them, having breastplates of fire, and of jacinth, and brimstone: and the heads of the horses were as the heads of lions; and out of their mouths issued fire and smoke and brimstone. By these three was the third part of men killed, by the fire, and by the smoke, and by the brimstone, which issued out of their mouths. For their power is in their mouth, and in their tails: for their tails were like unto serpents, and had heads, and with them they do hurt. And the rest of the men which were not killed by these plagues yet repented not of the works of their hands, that they should not worship devils, and idols of gold, and silver, and brass, and stone, and of wood: which neither can see, nor hear, nor walk: Neither repented they of their murders, nor of their sorceries, nor of their fornication, nor of their thefts."*

This judgment will probably be the last major war before the battle of Armageddon (War of wars). This massive warfare will be fought around the area of the Middle East (near the great river Euphrates). It will involve the modern-day armies of both Eastern and Western hemisphere nations. Many thousands and perhaps millions of both civilian and military personnel will die as a result of this awful war. This trumpet judgment will conclude the fourth seal. But though millions and billions of the world's population will perish through these awful calamities, many will still not repent. They will, on the contrary, harden their hearts and continue in their sinful lifestyles, shamelessly.

Chapter 6

Revealing the Fifth Seal

Revelation 6:9-11
"And when he had opened the fifth seal, I saw under the altar the souls of them that were slain for the word of God, and for the testimony which they held: And they cried with a loud voice, saying, How long, O Lord, holy and true, dost thou not judge and avenge our blood on them that dwell on the earth? And white robes were given unto every one of them; and it was said unto them, that they should rest yet for a little season, until their fellow servants also and their brethren, that should be killed as they were, should be fulfilled."

The previous four seals revealed the beginning of God's wrath (mixed with mercy) poured upon one third of earth's natural resources and its inhabitants. You may wonder, why was this wrath mixed with God's mercy? The reason for this is because His saints will still be dwelling here on earth to fulfill God's purposes. Once they have fulfilled and accomplished their purpose for being here, then this next seal will reveal how they will be removed from this earth. This fifth Seal deals exclusively with the Church and saints of the last days. Once again, the details for this seal are given to us by the seventh and final trumpet judgment.

THE SEVENTH TRUMPET JUDGMENT—*Revelation 10:7 "But in the days of the voice of the seventh angel, when he shall* begin *to sound, the mystery of God should be finished, as he hath declared to his servants the prophets." Revelation 11:14-18 "The second woe is past; and, behold, the* third woe *cometh quickly. And the seventh angel sounded; and there were great voices in heaven, saying, The kingdoms of this world are become the kingdoms of our Lord, and of his Christ; and he shall reign for ever and ever. And the four and twenty elders, which sat before God on their seats, fell upon their faces, and worshipped God, Saying, We give thee thanks, O LORD God Almighty, which art, and wast, and art to come; because thou hast taken to thee thy great power, and hast reigned. And the nations were angry, and thy wrath is come, and the time of the dead, that they should be judged, and that thou shouldest give* reward *unto thy servants the prophets, and to the saints, and them that fear thy name, small and great; and shouldest destroy them which destroy the earth."* (emphasis mine)

The first thing one must understand about this judgment is that, when this seventh and final trumpet is sounded, many events are going to transpire during the duration of this judgment. So please keep this in mind as we observe the following events:

THE FIRST EVENT

The first event we see unfolding, according to the scriptures, will be the final angelic war in the heavenlies between Michael and his angels against Satan and his fallen angels; *Revelation 12:7-11 "And there was war in heaven: Michael and his angels fought against the dragon; and the dragon fought and his angels, And prevailed not; neither was their place found any more in heaven. And the great dragon was cast out, that old serpent, called the Devil, and Satan, which deceiveth the whole world: he was cast out into the earth, and his angels were cast out with him. And I heard a loud voice saying in heaven, Now is come salvation, and strength, and the kingdom of our God, and the* power *of his Christ: for the accuser of our brethren is cast down, which accused them before our God day and night. And they overcame him by the blood of the Lamb, and by the word of their testimony; and they loved not their lives unto the death. Therefore rejoice, ye heavens, and ye that dwell in them.* Woe *to the inhabiters of the earth and of the sea! for the devil is come down unto you, having great wrath, because he knoweth that he hath but a short time."* (emphasis mine). This last woe is not so much directed only to sinners, but aimed especially at the saints.

THE SECOND EVENT

Once the Devil is finally cast out of the heavenly realm, he will descend with an insane anger and possess the body of the Antichrist; *Revelation 13:2 "And the beast which I saw was like unto a leopard, and his feet were as the feet of a bear, and his mouth as the mouth of a lion:* and the dragon gave him his power, and his seat, and great authority." (emphasis mine). He did this once, according to Luke's gospel, when he entered into the body of the first son of perdition, Judas Iscariot (*Luke 22:3*).

This physical possession will literally be the Devil incarnate. He will use this possession to imitate the true incarnation of the Son of God, Jesus Christ. Satan has always tried to emulate God's plan and purpose. Thus, by transforming himself into the body of the Antichrist, he will then present himself as the World's promised Messiah and Savior, deceiving the inhabitants (especially orthodox Jews) of the earth—except for the saints, of course. They will discern and know his true identity as the personification of evil.

Some teach that the reason the Antichrist cannot manifest himself yet, is because the Holy Spirit's dwelling (hindering force) within the Church, is preventing him from doing so.

They use this scriptural passage found in (*2 Thessalonians 2:7*) to justify their theory. Let's examine this verse a little bit more closely; *"For the mystery of iniquity doth <u>already</u> work: only he who now letteth will let, until he be taken out of the way."* They assume that the *he* mentioned in this verse refers to the Holy Spirit. But a closer examination of this verse in its original language does not confirm this. In its original context, it is just a simple pronoun, referring to an individual.

The individual that I believe it's referring to is none other than Michael, the archangel. As it's been already mentioned in the first event, he is the warrior angel who is seen hindering and battling Satan and his forces of darkness. He is probably the same angel that is presently responsible in restraining the rider of the red horse, from being released. Moreover, he is the angel who is always associated with end-time events, according to *Daniel 12:1;* *"And at that time shall Michael stand up, the great prince which standeth for the children of thy people: and there shall be a time of trouble, such as never was since there was a nation even to that same time: and at that time thy people shall be delivered, every one that shall be* found *written in the book."* When Michael (not the Church) is finally taken out of the way, then Satan will descend to earth to take possession of the Antichrist, in order to manifest himself *2 Thessalonians 2:8-12;* *"And then shall that Wicked be revealed, whom the Lord shall consume with the spirit of his mouth, and shall destroy with the brightness of his coming: Even him, whose coming is after the working of Satan with all power and signs and lying wonders, And with all deceivableness of unrighteousness in them that perish; because they* received *not the love of the truth, that they might be saved. And for this cause God shall send them strong delusion, that they should believe a lie: That they all might be damned who believed not the truth, but had pleasure in unrighteousness."*

THE THIRD EVENT

The Antichrist will officially then declares war on the saints and cause great persecution and tribulation to come upon the Church. He hates God, and the only way that he can retaliate is by hurting the Church that Jesus Christ established and loves (*Mark 3:13-19*). This attack of Satan will occur toward the end of the first three-and-a-half year segment of our final conflict with him. This is the evil day that Paul warned us about in *Ephesians 6:13*.

The Antichrist is going to be successful in putting the blame on the saints for all of the world's calamities and maladies. Today, since the awful attack of September 11, 2001 (twin tower tragedy in New York City), many American-born Arabs and Arabs in general, are held in high suspicion. The prejudice is not only held by other American citizens, but by other nations around the world. This suspicion is compounded and made worse if they are especially associated with the religion of Islam. Many have been unjustly accused of being terrorists, simply because they belong to that religion. Indeed, it is not popular today to be Arab or to have an Arab name in the United States. But all this will change in the near future. It will then be the Christians' turn to be branded not only as terrorists, but as a host of other derogatory names.

The devil-Antichrist will accuse the saints and use them as scapegoats for the tragic events that the world has been experiencing. Such events as famines, earthquakes, natural disasters, plagues, pestilence, wars, unthinkable crimes, riots, violence, human rights abuse, racism, local and regional electrical blackouts, environmental pollution of all types, unemployment, economic instability, and any other chaotic conditions that may exist will be blamed on the saints. The tragic result from this false accusation against the saints will produce violent hatred and attacks from people all over the world.

In that day, we will need God's grace and power to prepare our minds and hearts to endure this satanic hatred coming from the masses. Jesus predicted; *"Then shall they deliver you up to be afflicted, and shall kill you: and ye shall be hated of all nations for my name's sake"*. *"But he that shall* endure *unto the end, the same shall be saved" (Matthew 24:9, 13)*. The apostle Paul, in his epistle to the Philippians, stated the same thing in this manner *"And in nothing terrified by your adversaries: which is to them an evident* token *of perdition, but to you of salvation, and that of God. For unto you it is given in the behalf of Christ, not only to believe on him, but also to suffer for his sake" Philippians 1:28, 29.*

Saints, get ready to battle for your souls by putting on the whole armor of God (*Ephesians 6:10-18*). This final conflict that we're engaged in, between good and evil, life and death, heaven and hell, will become fiercer the closer we get to the coming of the Lord.

But the Church will be victorious in her final days, as she trusts in the wonderful promises of God, given to her in these passages of scriptures; *"These things I have spoken unto you, that in me ye might have peace. In the world ye shall have tribulation: but be of good cheer; I have overcome the world." John 16:33;* and again, *"Who shall separate us from the love of Christ? shall tribulation, or distress, or persecution, or famine, or nakedness, or peril, or sword? As it is written, For thy sake we are killed all the day long; we are accounted as sheep for the slaughter. Nay, in all these things we are more than conquerors through him that loved us. For I am persuaded, that neither death, nor life, nor angels, nor principalities, nor powers, nor things present, nor things to come, Nor height, nor depth, nor any other creature, shall be able to separate us from the love of God, which is in Christ Jesus our Lord" Romans 8:35-39.* Amen and Amen!

Paul the apostle, relates to us in his epistle to the church of Ephesus, that Christ is going to present to Himself, a glorious

Church (*Ephesians 5:26, 27*). The process that God has ordained for the Church to obtain this state of spiritual glory will be through both the washing of water by the Word and by the purifying fires of persecution. Please listen to the words of Christ, as He informs His disciples concerning this theme of persecution found in *John 15:18-20 "If the world hate you, ye know that it hated me before it hated you. If ye were of the world, the world would love his own: but because ye are not of the world, but I have chosen you out of the world, therefore the world hateth you. Remember the word that I said unto you, The servant is not greater than his lord. If they have persecuted me, they will also persecute you; if they have kept my saying, they will keep yours also."* Let us read what the prophet Daniel has to say in this regard, *"And some of them of understanding shall fall, to try them, and to* purge, *and to* make them white, *even to the time of the end: because it is yet for a time appointed."* (emphasis mine). And John said basically the same thing in, *Revelation 7:14 "And I said unto him, Sir, thou knowest. And he said to me, These are they which came out of great tribulation, and have* washed *their robes, and* made them white *in the blood of the Lamb."* (emphasis mine).

THE FOURTH EVENT

The next event will be the rise of the final false prophet, the Antichrist's right-hand man. He will be another diabolical being, who will be in charge of a one world religion. He will bring great deception upon the people of this planet by performing great signs and lying wonders. He will also produce, quite possibly, an image (human clone) of the Antichrist for worldwide worship. And finally, he will force everyone's allegiance to their totalitarian modern Babylonian system, by taking the mark of the beast—666 (*Revelation 13:11-18*). Many will take this mark, just to stay in the system. The main motive that will compel the masses to take this mark, will be, not only the fear of capital punishment, but ultimate selfishness (self, self, self).

What will this mark of the beast mean for all of the individuals living in that day when it is implemented? It will mean that without it, you will not be able to function anymore in your society and country. Many young people, as well as adults, will not be able to finish their education and begin their careers, or if adults, start a new career. You won't be able to pay anymore for entertainment or participate in any recreational activities that require a fee. You will not be able to continue your employment, or receive unemployment benefits if laid off. You won't have access to your bank accounts, no more retirement pensions, social security checks or insurance benefits; no health, dental, and vision insurance, no access to hospitals or clinics or be able to purchase pharmaceutical and nutritional products; no passports for travel, no business and property ownership; no way to pay for your mortgage, rental lease, utilities, and other household expenditures; no shopping at your favorite grocery store or supermarket, in order to feed yourself or family; no way to fuel your vehicles and machinery, no use of your HD television sets, computers, copiers, cell phones, and any wireless electronic gadgets, and so on.

The list can go on and on and on. So what will you do, when this mark is finally implemented by the false prophet? You will definitely need, in that day, a good dose of *faith and patience*, if you plan to survive those days, without taking the mark, "If *any man have an ear, let him hear. He that leadeth into captivity shall go into captivity: he that killeth with the sword must be killed with the sword.* Here is the patience and the faith of the saints" *Revelation 13:9, 10* (emphasis mine).

In that dreadful day, every human being will be forced and subjugated to accept the mark or face martyrdom. If you decide not to take this mark, then expect to be executed, mainly by being beheaded. The Lord will permit this baptism of suffering; *Matthew 20:22, 23; Revelation 20:4 "And I saw thrones, and they (twelve apostles),sat upon them, and judgment was given unto them: and I saw the souls of them that were beheaded for the witness of Jesus, and for the word of God, and which had not worshipped the beast, neither his image, neither had received his mark upon their foreheads, or in their hands; and they lived and reigned with Christ a thousand years"* (emphasis added).

Moreover, I would like to warn all those Christians who have been deceived by a prevalent, but erroneous doctrine: so-called eternal security. This teaching basically states that once a person gets genuinely saved, he or she can never lose their salvation. My warning to you is that, if you think you can take the mark of the beast and still keep your salvation, then you are deceived and you will seal your own doom (*Matthew 24:13; Hebrews 10:23-31; James 5:19, 20*).

God is going to press every human being living in that day to make a final decision. You will no longer be able to hypocritically have one foot in the world and one foot in the church. This mark will be the final separation between the brave sheep (Saints) and the cowardly goats (sinners), *Matthew 25:32, 33*.

Though this will be similar to a living nightmare, the Church and saints of the last days will be victorious in this regard according to; *Revelation 12:11; 15:2 "And they overcame him by the blood of the Lamb, and by the word of their testimony; and they loved not their lives unto the death"*. (emphasis mine) *"And I saw as it were a sea of glass mingled with fire (fiery trial): and them that had gotten the victory over the beast, and over his image, and over his mark, and over the number of his name, stand on the sea of glass, having the* harps *of God"* (emphasis added). The Bride's victory will be similar to the victory the house of Judah (Jews) experienced, many centuries ago in ancient Babylon. Please read this exciting story for yourself and be encouraged, about some individuals' refusal to worship a golden image and what it cost them for being courageous. It's recorded for us in *Daniel chapter 3*.

Note: please understand that by the time this particular event occurs, the Church will have already accomplished her three-and-a-half-year ministry, parallel to that of Christ. Similar to the way Jesus completed and fulfilled His three-and-a-half-year mission, so will the Church do likewise. Wherever the Head (Jesus) goes, the Body (Church) must follow.

Thus, once our Lord completed His ministry and fulfilled His Father's will here on earth, He was then turned over to His persecutors. The Jewish religious establishment (Sanhedrin Counsel) joined forces with the Roman political system of that day, and both condemned Him to death. It was the Jewish High priest and elders who sentenced Christ to death. But it was the Roman soldiers who did the dirty work of nailing Him to the cross. His suffering and subsequent death, was part of the foreordained plan of the Father for Him, *(Revelation 13:8)*.

Similarly, the Antichrist, representing the political system as President of presidents, will join forces with the religious establishment headed by the false prophet (modern High priest) and both will condemn the saints of the last days to their death. Peter the apostle, admonishes us in his first epistle with these words, *"For even hereunto were ye called: because Christ also suffered for us, leaving us an example, that ye should follow his steps: ..."* and again he says *"Be sober, be vigilant; because your adversary the devil, as a roaring lion, walketh about, seeking whom he may devour: Whom resist stedfast in the faith, knowing that the same afflictions are accomplished in your brethren that are in the world. But the God of all grace, who hath called us unto his eternal glory by Christ Jesus, after that ye have suffered a while, make you perfect, stablish, strengthen, settle you"* (*1 Peter 2:21; 5:8-10*). Amen and Amen!

This dark period for the Church is perhaps the night that Jesus referred to when He stated in, *John 9:4 "I must work the works of him that sent me, while it is day: the night cometh, when no man can work."* Indeed, this will be a time when the Church, having finished her mission, will have to probably go into hiding, similar to the way saints did in the past; *(Hebrews 11:33-40)*.

Here is another word of advice: if you do get the opportunity to escape and hide in some wilderness or remote area, please plan now to learn some outdoor survival skills. You will definitely need it in that day! Get ready to join the ranks of those that are foodless and homeless! Survival will be the name of that game. If you fail to plan, then you are planning to fail. Please take heed to the words of this wise preacher found in *Proverbs 22:3 "A prudent man foreseeth the evil, and hideth himself: but the simple pass on, and are punished."*

Maybe this is the reason why God will send, after some members (missionaries especially) of the Church go into hiding, three dynamic angels to continue announcing to the inhabitants of the earth, God's final message of mercy found in; *Revelation 14:6-13 " And I saw another angel fly in the midst of heaven, having the everlasting gospel to preach unto them that dwell on the earth, and to every nation, and kindred, and tongue, and people, Saying with a loud voice, Fear God, and give glory to him; for the hour of his judgment is come: and worship him that made heaven, and earth, and the sea, and the fountains of waters. And there followed another angel, saying, Babylon is fallen, is fallen, that great city, because she made all nations drink of the wine of the wrath of her fornication. And the third angel followed them, saying with a loud voice, If any man worship the beast and his image, and receive his mark in his forehead, or in his hand, The same shall drink of the wine of the wrath of God, which is poured out* without mixture into *the cup of his indignation; and he shall be tormented with fire and brimstone in the presence of the holy angels, and in the presence of the Lamb: And the smoke of their torment ascendeth up for ever and ever: and they have no rest day nor night, who worship the beast and his image, and whosoever receiveth the mark of his name. Here is the* patience of the saints: *here are they that keep the commandments of God, and the* faith of

Jesus. *And I heard a voice from heaven saying unto me, Write, Blessed are the dead which die in the Lord from henceforth: Yea, saith the Spirit, that they may rest from their labours; and their works do follow them."* (emphasis mine).

A final note, for some of the saints who might get the opportunity to hide and stay alive, Jesus predicted that the world would try to entice some to come out of their hiding places when He stated in *Matthew 24:26 "Wherefore if they shall say unto you, Behold, he is in the desert; go not forth: behold, he is in the secret chambers; believe it not."* They will use technology against you, especially satellites, which are basically spies in the sky to detect your hiding place.

But Christ made it real clear to His disciples, what particular sign they needed to be aware of, that would indicate His soon arrival. The sign is given to us by John's vision in *Revelation 6:12* which states; *"And I beheld when he had opened the sixth seal, and, lo, there was a great earthquake; and the sun became black as sackcloth of hair, and the moon became as blood;"*

Yes, depending in what part of the world you are living at that time, if it's during the day time, then the sun will become pitch black. But if it's during the night, then the moon will darken that side of the world, by becoming bloody red. The next light that you and the world will behold will be, the glorious light of our blessed Lord and Savior, Jesus Christ, at His coming; *"For as the lightning cometh out of the east, and shineth even unto the west; so shall also the coming of the Son of man be" Matthew 24:27.* Praise God!

Today we have a carnally weak, lukewarm, and prayerless Church that thinks she is going to escape the wrath of the Antichrist through a pretribulation rapture. This pretribulation rapture mentality, which I oppose, has done more to harm the Church in the areas of discipleship and maturity, than anyone could ever imagine. Nothing has done more to disarm and prevent the preparation of the Church for her *final conflict*, than this distorted man-made theory of an easy rapture. It sounds good, but this was not the way the doctrine of the first resurrection was taught by the Early Church. It gives the present day church a false confidence that they will not have to face tribulation.

On the contrary, their theory sounds more like a fable, produced by misguided teachers who are more concern about pleasing people, than teaching truth. They misinterpret and pull scriptures out of context to justify the timing of their doctrine of escapism. I sometimes reflect and hope they are right in their teaching and I'm wrong in mine, because I do not relish the thought of suffering, but I don't think I am.

Paul warns us about these teachers, with these sobering words, *"I charge thee therefore before God, and the Lord Jesus Christ, who shall judge the quick and the dead at his appearing and his kingdom; Preach the word; be instant in season, out of season; reprove, rebuke, exhort with all long suffering and doctrine. For the time will come when* they will not endure sound doctrine; *but after their own lusts shall they heap to themselves teachers, having itching ears; And they shall turn away their ears from the truth, and shall be turned unto fables"* 2 Timothy 4:1-4 (emphasis mine). The apostle Peter also stated in his second epistle that false teachers would become rich, by taking advantage of Christians scriptural ignorance; *2 Peter 2:1-3 "But there were false prophets also among the people, even as there shall be false teachers among you, who privily shall bring in damnable heresies, even denying the Lord that bought them, and bring upon themselves swift destruction. And many shall follow their pernicious ways; by reason of whom the way of truth shall be evil spoken of. And through covetousness shall they with feigned words make merchandise of you: whose judgment now of a long time lingereth not, and their damnation slumbereth not."*

To add to this, Jesus predicted some sad consequences for Christians who were not prepared to face these coming hard times of persecution and martyrdom. *"And then shall many be offended, and shall betray one another, and shall hate one another. And many false prophets shall rise, and shall deceive many. And because iniquity shall abound, the love of many shall wax cold. But he that shall endure unto the end, the same shall be saved" (Matthew 24:10-13).* I do not know if you agree or disagree with this point of view. But I would rather paint a worst-case scenario than to give Christians a false hope about not being here to experience the first five seals, at least, described in the apocalyptic book of Revelation.

If what I've been sharing all along is nothing close to God's will for us, then I stand guilty for just adding unnecessary anxiety and distress to your life. We will just fly away and live happily ever after! If what I'm saying is true, however, and you have been teaching otherwise, then you will stand guilty for misleading all the people who heard you, and their blood will be in your hands (Ezekiel 33:1-9).

THE FIFTH EVENT

This final and glorious event will conclude the seventh trumpet judgment. After the Church has accomplished her mission, been judged, purged, and perfected through persecution (2 Peter 4:12-19; 2 Thessalonians1:3-5), She will, in a matter of a few days or weeks, be quickly delivered—raptured—from this earth. The apostle Paul, in his first letter to the church at Corinth relates to us that this first resurrection (rapture) event was a hidden mystery unveiled to him.

On a personal note, the illumination of this passage of scripture, for this author, was a catalyst in my search and research for a better understanding of this particular trumpet. The scripture passage I'm referring to, is found in *1 Corinthians 15:51, 52: "Behold, I shew you a mystery; We shall not all sleep, but we shall all be changed, In a moment, in the twinkling of an eye,* at the last trump: *for the trumpet shall sound, and the dead shall be raised incorruptible, and we shall be changed* [emphasis mine]."

Now, this passage of scripture clearly shows us when the rapture will occur, which will be at the sound of the final, or last, trumpet. I reasoned, meditated, and pondered on these verses for a long time, until God enlightened my understanding of it. He simply revealed to me that if there is a last trumpet, then obviously there must be other trumpets that precede it.

To my surprise, I discovered that not only did Paul relate the timing of the Church's first resurrection to the final trumpet, but so did our blessed Lord and Savior, Jesus Christ and His beloved apostle John. Yes, Jesus relates, in the Gospels, the final trumpet with the rapture, which we will look at in a moment. But it is in John's apocalyptic vision that we see the other series of trumpets leading to this final trumpet. Praise the Lord!

Let us now take a closer look at these scriptural passages that deal with this final trumpet:

1. THE FINAL TRUMPET OR RAPTURE, ACCORDING TO CHRIST
   A. *"Immediately after the tribulation* (persecution) *of those days shall the sun be darkened, and the moon shall not give her light, and the stars shall fall from heaven, and the powers of the heavens shall be shaken: And then shall appear the sign of the Son of man in heaven: and then shall all the tribes of the earth mourn, and they shall see the Son of man coming in the clouds of heaven with power and great glory. And he shall send his angels with a* great sound of a trumpet, *and they shall gather together his elect from the four winds, from one end of heaven to the other." Matthew 24:29-31* (emphasis added)
   B. *"And then shall they see the Son of man coming in the clouds with great power and glory. And then shall he send his angels, and shall gather together his elect from*

the four winds, from the uttermost part of the earth to the uttermost part of heaven." Mark 13:26, 27
C. *"And then shall they see the Son of man coming in a cloud with power and great glory. And when these things begin to come to pass, then look up, and lift up your heads; for your redemption (rapture) draweth nigh." Luke 21:26, 27* (emphasis added)

2. THE FINAL TRUMPET OR RAPTURE, ACCORDING TO PAUL
    A. *"Behold, I shew you a mystery; We shall not all sleep, but we shall allbe changed, in a moment, in the twinkling of an eye, at the last trump: for the trumpet shall sound, and the dead shall be raised incorruptible, and we shall be changed." 1 Corinthians 15:51, 52*
    B. *"For this we say unto you by the word of the Lord, that we which arealive and remain unto the coming of the Lord shall not prevent them which are asleep. For the Lord himself shall descend from heaven* with a shout, with the voice of the archangel, *and with the* trump of God: *and the dead in Christ shall rise first: Then we which are alive and remain shall be caught up together with them in the clouds, to meet the Lord in the air: and so shall we ever be with the Lord. Wherefore comfort one another with these words" 1 Thessalonians 4:15-18* (emphasis mine).

3. THE FINAL TRUMPET OR RAPTURE, ACCORDING TO JOHN
    A. *"But in the days of the voice of the seventh angel, when he shall* begin*to sound, the mystery of God (Christ and His Church, Ephesians 5:32) should be finished, as he hath declared to his servants the prophets." Revelation 10:7* (emphasis added)

B. *"And I looked, and behold a white cloud, and upon* the cloud *one sat like unto the Son of man, having on his head a golden crown, and in his hand a sharp sickle. And another* angel *came out of the temple,* crying with a loud voice *to him that sat on the cloud, Thrust in thy sickle, and reap; for the time is come for thee to reap; for the harvest of the earth is ripe. And he that sat on the cloud thrust in his sickle on the earth; and the earth was reaped." Revelation 14:14-16* (emphasis mine).

So, as we observe these passages of scripture, especially this last one of John, we come to the conclusion that the rapture of the Church occurs, not in the beginning of *Revelation* chapter 4, as some erroneously teach, but toward the middle of the book, in chapter 14. From this point on, the Church is seen in chapter 15, rejoicing in heaven, for having overcome the beast, the mark, and his modern Babylonian system.

Here is a wonderful scene from this chapter, *"And I saw as it were a sea of glass mingled with fire: and them that had gotten the victory over the beast, and over his image, and over his mark, and over the number of his name, stand on the sea of glass, having the* harps *of God. And they sing the song of Moses the servant of God, and the song of the Lamb, saying, Great and marvellous are thy works, Lord God Almighty; just and true are thy ways, thou King of saints. Who shall not fear thee, O Lord, and glorify thy name? for thou only art holy: for all nations shall come and worship before thee; for thy judgments are made manifest." Revelation 15:2-4 Hallelujah and Amen!*

CHAPTER 7

Revealing the Sixth Seal

Revelation 6:12-17
"And I beheld when he had opened the sixth seal, and, lo, there was a great earthquake; and the sun became black as sackcloth of hair, and the moon became as blood; And the stars of heaven fell unto the earth, even as a fig tree casteth her untimely figs, when she is shaken of a mighty wind. And the heaven departed as a scroll when it is rolled together; and every mountain and island were moved out of their places. And the kings of the earth, and the great men, and the rich men, and the chief captains, and the mighty men, and every bondman, and every free man, hid themselves in the dens and in the rocks of the mountains; And said to the mountains and rocks, Fall on us, and hide us from the face of him that sitteth on the throne, and from the wrath of the Lamb: For the great day of his wrath is come; and who shall be able to stand?"

This final seal of judgment represents the dreadful "Day of the Lord" (*Isaiah 13:6-13*) and the fullness of God's wrath. The judgments of this awful seal and the drastic events that proceed from it are going to cause tremendous fear, horror, and terror for the remaining unrepentant sinful inhabitants of this earth. The times of the gentiles to be saved will be fulfilled, when the rapture of the saints occurs (*Romans 11:11, 12, 25*). Forget that *false belief* of Christians being left behind after the rapture. Either you participate in that first resurrection-rapture or consider yourself doomed for eternity; *Revelation 20:6* *"Blessed and holy is he that hath part in the first resurrection: on such the second death hath no* power, *but they shall be priests of God and of Christ, and shall reign with him a thousand years."*

Thus, like I've mentioned already in my explanation of the fifth seal, the glorious second coming of Christ will have a two-fold effect upon the people of this world. For the surviving saints, it will be a great time of elation and rejoicing! The saints will know that the day of their departure has finally arrived, but for the remaining wicked, it will be the terror of terrors!

The terrifying effect of the appearance of Christ coming in the clouds will cause many to panic in fear and run to the dens and mountains (hidden bases), in order to hide themselves from Him (*Isaiah 2:17-22*). But Jesus stated to the disciples, in His Olivet discourse, that they will not escape; *Luke 21:32-35* *"Verily I say unto you, This generation shall not pass away, till all be fulfilled. Heaven and earth shall pass away: but my words shall not pass away. And take heed to yourselves, lest at any time your hearts be overcharged with surfeiting, and drunkenness, and cares of this life, and so that day come upon you unawares.* For as a snare shall it come on all them that dwell on the face of the whole earth." (emphasis mine). Now the world will see and fear the awesome power of God Almighty!

THE FINAL SEVEN PLAGUES OF JUDGMENT

Beginning with *Revelation* chapter 15 verses 5-8, and continuing through chapter 16, we behold seven angels with seven golden vials, full of the wrath of God. The following list, will give you a brief description of what these seven golden vials or plagues are.

First Plague:	Grievous sore upon the human race	Revelation 16:1, 2
Second Plague:	The Sea becomes as blood	" 16:3
Third Plague:	The rivers turn into blood	" 16:4-7
Fourth Plague:	The sun scorches mankind	" 16:8, 9
Fifth Plague:	Darkness over the beast's dominion	" 16:10, 11
Sixth Plague:	The battle of Armageddon	" 16:12-16

This final battle of Armageddon, which I call the war of wars, needs some explaining. We will need to look at some prior events that will lead to this final battle. These events will transpire during the second three-and-a-half-year segment.

To begin, upon the rapture of the Church, which means the fulfillment of the Gentiles and converted Jews salvation, God will resume His dealings exclusively with the Jewish people who have returned to the land of Palestine. More specifically, He will deal with the orthodox Jews in particular. The secular and liberal Jews will have already given their allegiance to this false messiah (Antichrist) by taking his mark upon their foreheads and right hands, *Revelation 13:16*.

Once this false messiah (Antichrist) manifests his true colors of deception, the orthodox Jews will finally realize that they have been duped, all along. Their eyes will be opened when they behold this diabolical beast desecrate their rebuilt modern Temple and by his proclamation of being superior to their God; *Daniel 9:27; 12:11; Matthew 24:15; 2 Thessalonians 2:3, 4*.

It is during this time that God will supernaturally send down to earth His two olive trees (also known as witnesses and prophets). These two individuals will probably be Moses and

Elijah. The reason I say this is because they are seen together on the "Mount of Transfiguration," talking to Christ about His decease; *Luke 9:28-36*.

Moreover, these two individuals are highly respected and honored among orthodox Jews. That is because Moses represents the letter of their Law and Elijah, the spirit of their Law, as the prophet of prophets.

Their mission and ministry on earth will be exclusively focused on the Jewish people, in the land of Palestine. Only these deceived orthodox Jews will be given an opportunity by God to repent and discover their true Messiah, Jesus Christ, the Son of the Living God; *Matthew 16:13-18*. According to *Revelation 11:1-13*, a remnant of these orthodox Jews will be converted, as a result of their prophesying.

Once these two witnesses finish their testimony, the Antichrist will be permitted to kill them. He kills them because these two prophets, through their preaching, will have tormented him and the inhabitants of this world. A sign of a true prophet or prophetess is the type of message that they proclaim. Does the message disturb and torment people in their sinful condition? Or does the message please, tickle, and allow sinners to remain in their lost condition, like the messages of phony prophets do?

The Antichrist will then rally the armies of the world to totally annihilate and wipe out Israel and the remnant from the face of this earth, in the battle of Armageddon; *Revelation 16:12-14, 16*. It is at this time that Christ returns to this earth with the armies of heaven to rescue the remnant, defeat the Antichrist with his brainwashed armies and finally set up His earthly Kingdom; *Revelation 17:11-14; 19:11-21*.

Seventh Plague: A great earthquake, the condemnation of the modern Babylonian system and a great, heavy hail storm—*16:17-21*

The final details of the destruction of this modern Babylonian system are given to us in chapters *17, 18,* and part of chapter *19:11-21*. By reading these chapters, one will discover that this modern Babylonian system is satanic in its origin. This is the satanic system that manipulates and drives nations behind the scenes. The nations and peoples of this earth do not realize that they are being played upon by an organized unseen demonic force. Paul the apostle describes this satanic system as the "mystery of iniquity" (*2 Thessalonians 2:7*).

This mystery of iniquity has been with us, since the beginning of time. It first manifested itself in the Garden of Eden when it deceived Eve and caused her to sin. It also eventually caused Adam to sin. It then manifested its ugly head again when it caused Cain to slay (kill) his brother, Able. And finally, this mystery of iniquity enveloped the whole known world. Its corruption spread throughout the world to the point that God had to eventually destroy it, with the deluge (flood).

Today, we once again see this antichrist, anti-God, anti-family, and anti-Church spirit, operating in full force, through this modern Babylonian system. What in reality is this system? Why should we be concerned about it?

This so-called modern Babylon, as John saw it, is basically a religious, philosophical, political, economic, military, and totalitarian system that Satan has set up. The enemy has had six thousand years of experience, dealing with the human race. This system is nothing new for him. He attempted this once in the past by using Nimrod (the first Antichrist) and the tower of Babel to set up his world order in opposition to God's will. But God disrupted it! Read it for yourself in *Genesis 11*.

The modern system that is being implemented today is called the New World Order. John was able to see this future system for what it really is and compared it to ancient Babylon. This modern Babylonian system will prepare the stage for the manifestation of the final Antichrist. He will use this totalitarian system to enslave and control the nations and peoples of this world. This Godless and humanistic system will eventually also face the destructive judgment of God, according to this seventh plague. This is the reason why we need to be concerned.

We should be concerned about getting ourselves so entangled with this system, to the point that we cannot free ourselves from it. Remember that we are in the world but not a part of it. This world is not our final home, but as strangers and pilgrims, we're just passing through. Our final home that awaits us is a glorious golden city called the New Jerusalem prepared by our Lord Jesus Christ, *"Let not your heart be troubled: ye believe in God, believe also in me. In my Father's house are many mansions: if it were not so, I would have told you. I go to prepare a place for you. And if I go and prepare a place for you, I will come again, and receive you unto myself; that where I am, there ye may be also." John 14:1-3* and also, *Revelation 21:1, 2 "And I saw a new heaven and a new earth: for the first heaven and the first earth were passed away; and there was no more sea. And I John saw the holy city, new Jerusalem, coming down from God out of heaven, prepared as a bride adorned for her husband."*

Why should we still be concerned about modern Babylon? Because this modern Babylonian system of total darkness and its main pagan city are going to experience the fullness of God's wrath. But before He pours out His fury upon the sins of this satanic system and its Babylonian City, He will summon His people out of it; *Revelation 18:1-6 "And after these things I saw another angel come down from heaven, having great power; and the earth was lightened with his glory. And he cried mightily with a strong voice, saying, Babylon the great is fallen, is fallen, and is become the habitation of devils, and the hold of every foul spirit, and a cage of every unclean and hateful bird. For all nations have drunk of the wine of the wrath of her fornication, and the kings of the earth have committed fornication with her, and the merchants of the earth are waxed rich through the abundance of her delicacies. And I heard another voice from heaven, saying,* Come out of her, my people, *that ye be not partakers of her sins, and that ye receive not of her plagues. For her sins have reached unto heaven, and God hath remembered her iniquities. Reward her even as she rewarded you, and double unto her double according to her works: in the cup which she hath filled fill to her double."* (emphasis mine).

The call that has been upon this Church age for approximately two thousand years has been this call to come out of the world's Babylonian systems. This call to come out will become more intense, the closer we get to the coming of our Lord. Though Babylon is made up of many different systems all working together, such as politics, philosophies, economies, and so forth, the main arena that should concern us is the area of religion.

This Babylonian one-world religion, which I mentioned before in chapter 6, will have a Babylonian world Church. This false Church is described in *Revelation Chapters 17 and 18* as a decorated harlot and prostitute. The reason she is described this way is because she adulterates (through her man-made traditions) the purity of God's Word and fornicates with the systems of this world. The peoples of this world are made drunk and are also duped by the wine of the wrath of her fornication. This religious system will consist of all of the major and minor religions of the world. Even some Roman Catholics, Eastern Orthodox, Protestant mainline denominations, Evangelicals, classical Pentecostal and Charismatic groups, and other apostate religious organizations and cults will unite (ecumenical movement) to form this super false religious system.

This false so-called super Church will be responsible for the persecution and martyrdom (modern inquisition) of God's true Church and saints. But God will eventually avenge the blood of His servants, by destroying this false religious entity. This system of religion is headed for doom and destruction; *Revelation 17:16-18 "And the ten horns which thou sawest upon the beast, these shall hate the whore, and shall make her desolate and naked, and shall eat her flesh, and burn her with fire.*

For God hath put in their hearts to fulfil his will, and to agree, *and give their kingdom unto the beast, until the words of God shall be fulfilled. And the woman which thou sawest is that great city, which reigneth over the kings of the earth."* Read also *Revelation 18:7-24*.

Now whether John, in his vision of the future, was referring to the destruction of this Babylonian City, to Vatican City, or some other major city, I cannot say, at this time. But rest assure that whatever city he is referring to, it would have to be a city that has first, a long historical record of persecuting and killing God's apostles, prophets, and saints. Second, it would have to be a city that has access to the sacred scriptures, where one can still hear the voice of the Bridegroom and the voice of the Bride in it. And finally, it would have to be a city that uses sorcery (ceremonial incantations) to seduce, bewitch, and mesmerize its citizens (followers). I will let you figure that one out for yourself.

So, Saints, please heed the Call of God and Come Out of her!

Begin to come out of her, politically;
Begin to come out of her, philosophically;
Begin to come out of her, culturally;
Begin to come out of her, commercially;
Begin to come out of her, economically;
Begin to come out of her, militarily;
But most importantly, begin to come out her, religiously!

Therefore, you and I must come out of this Babylonian system, not by leaving Planet Earth, but by coming out of it in our heart, soul and mind. Please look at these passages of scripture; *1 John 2: 15-17; "Love not the world, neither the things that are in the world. If any man love the world, the love of the Father is not in him. For all that is in the world, the lust of the flesh, and the lust of the eyes, and the pride of life, is not of the Father, but is of the world.*

And the world passeth away, and the lust thereof: but he that doeth the <u>will of God</u> abideth for ever."

James 4:4 "Ye adulterers and adulteresses, know ye not that the friendship of the world is enmity with God? whosoever therefore will be a friend of the world is the enemy of God."

2 Corinthians 6:14-18 "Be ye not unequally yoked together with unbelievers: for what fellowship hath righteousness with unrighteousness? And what communion hath light with darkness?

And what concord hath Christ with Belial? Or what part hath he that believeth with an infidel? And what agreement hath the temple of God with idols? For ye are the temple of the living God; as God hath said, I will dwell in them, and walk in them; and I will be their God, and they shall be my people. Wherefore come out from among them, *and be ye separate, saith the Lord, and touch not the unclean thing; and I will receive you. And will be a Father unto you, and ye shall be my sons and daughters, saith the Lord Almighty." ; Matthew 6:19-21 "Lay not up for yourselves treasures upon earth, where moth and rust doth corrupt, and where thieves break through and steal: But lay up for yourselves treasures in heaven, where neither moth nor rust doth corrupt, and where thieves do not break through nor steal:* For where your treasure is, there will your heart be also." (emphasis mine)

Colossians 3:1-3 "If ye then be risen with Christ, seek those things which are above, where Christ sitteth on the right hand of God. Set your affection on things above, *not on things on the earth. For ye are dead, and your life is hid with Christ in God."*(emphasis mine).

Now obviously, if we are called to come out of this false religious (church) system, then we will need to go into and become part of another entity. God's call for us today is to unite with the true Church of God. One of the main purposes for Christ first advent to this earth was for Him to build His organic (flesh and blood) Church and then die for it; Acts 20:28 *"Take heed therefore unto yourselves, and to all the flock, over the which the Holy Ghost hath made you overseers, to feed the church of God, which he hath purchased with his own blood."* He first built the nucleus of this Church, by choosing twelfth of His closes disciples from the company of disciples, whom He named afterward, apostles (*Luke 6:12-17*).

He then compared this nucleus of apostles to a sheepfold. A sheepfold that He would eventually use to rally all of His true sheep (Saints) into. How will the true sheep know where this fold is located today? They will know by listening and following the voice of the true Shepherd. Not a stranger's voice, but a familiar voice. Yes, a voice that would be gentle, yet powerful and full of truth. *John 10:2-6, 14-16; "But he that entereth in by the door is the shepherd of the sheep. To him the porter openeth; and the sheep hear his voice: and he calleth his own sheep by name, and leadeth them out. And when he putteth forth his own sheep, he goeth before them, and the sheep follow him:* for they know his voice. *And a stranger will they not follow, but will flee from him:* for they know not the voice of strangers." And *"I am the good shepherd, and* know my sheep, *and* am known of mine. *As the Father knoweth me, even so know I the Father: and I lay down my life for the sheep. And* other sheep I have, *which are not of this fold: them also I must bring, and* they shall hear my voice; *and* there shall be one fold, *and* one shepherd." (emphasis mine).

Furthermore, when Jesus was being interrogated by Pontius Pilate (a Roman Procurator), He made an ultimate defense for the truth. Let's read this interesting conversation that went on, between the two of them. *John 18:33-38, "Then Pilate entered into the judgment hall again, and called Jesus, and said unto him, Art thou the King of the Jews? Jesus answered him, Sayest thou this thing of thyself, or did others tell it thee of me? Pilate answered, Am I a Jew? Thine own nation and the chief priests have delivered thee unto me: what hast thou done? Jesus answered, My kingdom is not of this world: if my kingdom were of this world, then would my servants fight, that I should not be delivered to the Jews: but now is my kingdom not from hence. Pilate therefore said unto him, Art thou a king then? Jesus answered, Thou sayest that I am a king. To this end was I born, and for this cause came I into the world*, that I should bear witness unto the truth. Every one that is of the truth heareth my voice. *Pilate saith unto him, What is truth? And when he had said this, he went out again unto the Jews, and saith unto them, I find in him no fault at all."* (emphasis mine).

Notice that toward the end of this conversation, Pilate puts forth the question to Christ, *"What is truth?" John 18:38a.* The response he received from Christ was total silence. This intelligent Roman Procurator did not realize that truth was standing right before his very face. For Christ is the personification of truth! *John 1:1, 14; "In the beginning was the Word, and the Word was with God, and the Word was God. And the Word was made flesh, and dwelt among us, (and we beheld his glory, the glory as of the only begotten of the Father,) full of grace and truth."*

Jesus Himself stated emphatically, categorically and unequivocally that He is, *"... the way, the truth, and the life: no man cometh unto the Father, but by me." John 14:6.* This statement of truth alone should remind us that it was this gospel of truth, that saved us (*Ephesians 1:13*). Then we proceeded on to a subsequent experience of sanctification by the same truth (*2*

Thessalonians 2:13). And finally, we were spiritually baptized by Christ, with the Spirit of truth (*John 16:13*).

Christ, who is the living Truth, finally committed His oracles of truth, to the Church He established. The Church is now the custodian of this written truth. Paul the apostle, describes this custodian in these terms, *"But if I tarry long, that thou mayest know how thou oughtest to behave thyself in the house of God, which is the church of the living God, the pillar and ground of the truth" 1 Timothy 3:15*. And though the church is the pillar and ground of the truth, she does not produce this truth, but rather keeps, guards, and displays it (*John 17:6, 8*).

The truth that the Church is responsible to guard and protect is the entire Canon of the Bible (Holy Scriptures), which consists of both Old and New Testaments or Covenants. During this era that we're now living in, known as the dispensation of grace, she is especially committed to the New Testament. All members who have become part of God's true Church have made a verbal affirmation or declaration (pact) to faithfully uphold the terms of this New Covenant (*2 Corinthians 11:2, 3*). Just like Eve was deceived by Satan to abandon truth, so Paul's warning to that local church and to us is, don't fall into the spirit of apostasy (*2 Thessalonians 2:3*).

Seek out those fellowships and sheepfolds (churches) that have not compromised God's Word, but are still committed to the truth, the whole truth, and nothing but the truth. Christ gave His disciples this promise, which is still relevant for us today found in, *Luke 11:9, 10 "And I say unto you, Ask, and it shall be given you; seek, and ye shall find; knock, and it shall be opened unto you.*

For every one that asketh receiveth; and he that seeketh findeth; and to him that knocketh it shall be opened." I am not advocating for anyone to join the present religious organization that I belong to or any other particular pentecostal denomination, for all have been stained to one degree or another by Babylon. What I am advocating is for you to find a Church that is desperately trying to free itself from this Babylonian system and to be totally restored to the New Testament pattern of living. Pray earnestly with your whole heart to God, and He will graciously guide you into a haven (sheepfold) of truth. Praise God!

CHAPTER 8

Revealing the Seventh Seal

Revelation 8:1
"And when he had opened the seventh seal,
there was silence in heaven about the space of half an hour."

We finally arrive at this Seventh Seal, which is the last seal in this series. This seal is especially unique among the other seals, because it is not a seal representing judgment, but rather peace and rest. This seal is simply described by this one verse of scripture. It doesn't give us much information to elaborate on, so anyone who attempts to expound on this verse can only speculate. What stands out in this particular seal though is the number seven. And if you can recall, I've mentioned in my introduction that this number seven basically represents perfection, completion, and may I now add, rest.

My personal opinion and speculation is that this Seventh Seal represents the thousand-year period called the millennium. Why do I believe that this is what it represents? In *Genesis 2:2, 3;* we read, *"And on the seventh day God ended his work which he had made; and he rested on the seventh day from all his work which he had made.*

And God blessed the seventh day, and sanctified it: because that in it he had rested from all his work which God created and made." The apostle Peter tells us that, *"But, beloved, be not ignorant of this one thing, that one day is with the Lord as a thousand years, and a thousand years as one day." 2 Peter 3:8.* We read in *Genesis* that God sanctified the seventh day and made it a day of rest. And since a day according to Peter, is considered a thousand years to the Lord, then we can easily conclude that this Seventh Seal represents the millennial rest and reign of the Prince of Peace, Jesus Christ.

God has been working His plan of redemption and dealing with the human race for approximately six thousand years. Contrary to those who believe in the theory of evolution, man has only been around for a few thousand and not millions of years. Once Christ finishes His work of judging the world with the seven last plagues, then He will return to earth and establish His millennial kingdom; *Revelation 16:17 "And the seventh angel poured out his vial into the air; and there came a great voice out of the temple of heaven, from the throne, saying, It is done."*

As we read and begin to contemplate this one verse, we notice that John says that there is going to be silence in heaven, for one half hour. What does this silence mean? Again, I am only speculating but I think it means the following. The reason why there was silence in heaven, according to a minister I heard say in jest, was because all of the female saints will return with Christ, down to this earth. Ha, ha, ha, he was just joking of course! That is definitely not the reason for the silence in heaven. There won't be any female or male saints, just saints in heaven.

I believe the answer to this question can be found in the words of Christ, Himself. Jesus explicitly stated to His disciples that when He returns back to earth, He will come with all of His holy angels; *Matthew 25:31 "When the Son of man shall come in his glory, and all the holy angels with him, then shall he sit upon the throne of his glory:"* We know that one of the main activities of these holy angels that dwell in heaven, besides being messengers and warriors, is to worship and praise their Blessed Creator. They are constantly doing this, day and night. So obviously, when they temporarily leave heaven with Christ, then and only then will heaven be silent. That is when the silence comes into the picture.

The half hour, however long that might be, according to God's timetable, will be sufficient time to set up Christ's kingdom. Moreover, we know that not only the holy angels return with Christ, but also His Bride. This Bride will consist of only those saints who were called, chosen and faithful, here on earth *(Revelation 17:14)*. The Bride (Church) will be assisted by these holy angels, in the establishment of Christ's millennial earthly kingdom.

Once this task is completed, then these holy angels will be released to return to heaven and break that silence, as they resume their ministry of praise and worship. The Church (Bride, Queen) will remain here on earth to reign with Christ (Bridegroom, King) and to celebrate their thousand-year Holy honeymoon, *(Revelation 20:4-6)*. Hallelujah and Amen!

The following is a brief outline of some of the wonderful things that will take place, during this thousand-year time of rest and peace:

1. The present city of Jerusalem will be Christ's Headquarters; *Isaiah 2:1-3;Zechariah 14:4*.
2. No more weapons of warfare; *Isaiah 2:4*
3. Peace among the animal kingdom; *Isaiah 11:6-9*
4. People will live for a long time; *Isaiah 65:17-25*

Conclusion

The remaining chapters of the book of *Revelation* reveal the eternal state of the redeemed saints. It especially reveals a glorious City called "New Jerusalem", which has been purposely prepared by God, for His faithful servants that have overcome. I hope to be there someday!

Nevertheless, I trust these keys of illumination, which I have shared throughout this book, have helped to unlock your understanding of these *Seven Seals*. The insight you have gained from reading these pages should encourage and motivate you to prepare for what's coming ahead. Indeed, these are exciting as well as dangerous times we're living in.

Please understand that everyone living during the unveiling of these *Seven Seals* will suffer to one degree or another. I cannot emphasize this enough, but both saints and sinners will suffer together the first, second, third, and fourth seals. The sufferings of the fifth seal are exclusively reserved for the saints. Likewise, the sufferings of the sixth seal are reserved for the sinners who have rejected the love of the truth.

The decision you make today, will determine which suffering you will participate in. Either you suffer the wrath of the Antichrist by rejecting his satanic Babylonian system or you suffer the wrath of God Almighty by embracing the Antichrist system. The choice is yours to make!

Finally, my reason in writing this book was not to gain any recognition or popularity for myself. For the message contained in this book is obviously not popular. My main motive was to deliver the burden that God placed within my heart; a burden that involved warning and admonishing His people of these future events. If one or two or a few saints have been helped by this information in any way, then my joy and labor is fulfilled.

I now leave you with the words of a valiant warrior by the name of Joshua; *"Now therefore fear the* LORD, *and serve him in sincerity and in truth: and put away the gods which your fathers served on the other side of the flood, and in Egypt; and serve ye the* LORD.

And if it seem evil unto you to serve the LORD, *choose you this day whom ye will serve; whether the gods which your fathers served that were on the other side of the flood, or the gods of the Amorites, in whose land ye dwell: but as for me and my house, we will serve the* LORD.*" Joshua 24:14, 15.*

Conclusion

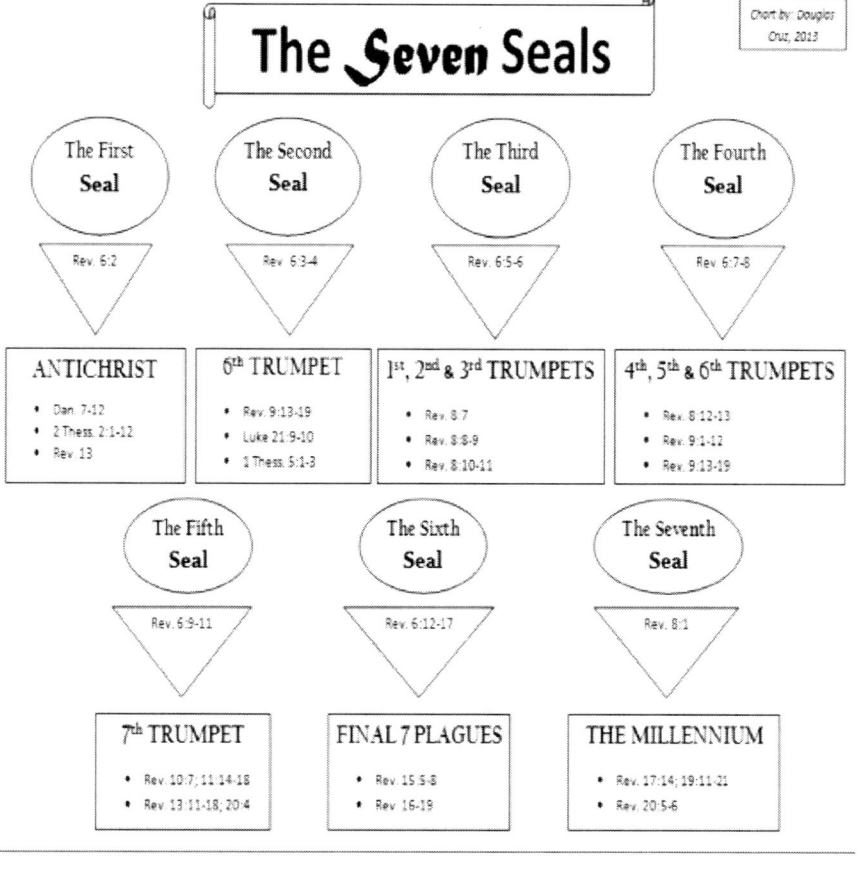

YOUR STORY

Your story, not mine, is one that has passed through the ages ...

Your story, not mine, is one written in books within countless pages ...

Your story is one of mercy and grace from above.

The reason, which you sent your only begotten Son to us with love ...

I deserve nothing good and do not know why you even give me of your time ...

Yet I hear your voice say, "My son, your story is part of mine.

So tell our story to others. Live each day for me.

For soon it will be time to come home and be with me ...

For all eternity."

Reginaldo "Reggie" Duarte Jr.

ABOUT THE AUTHOR

Douglas Cruz is a native of New York City (Spanish Harlem). His parents emigrated there from the Island of Puerto Rico during the 1940's. He was born on September 22, 1955. He was converted in November of 1973 and joined the Church of God of Prophecy in the summer of 1976. He answered the call to preach and was licensed as an evangelist in 1985 and ordained in 1992.

He has served the Church in several capacities. His pastorates include: Brussels, Belgium 1986-89; Yuma, Arizona 1990-92; Pahrump (Hispanic Congregation) and Las Vegas (English Congregation), Nevada 1992-93. He organized a bilingual local church during the year of 1994; that he still pastors in Fresno, California.

He served as Belgium national youth leader in 1986-88. Since 1992 he has been a district overseer (Arizona/Nevada) that year as well as a pastor. He has also directed Family Camps in the state of California since 2001

He attended and graduated from Bible Training Institute, Cleveland, Tennessee. He also attended Arizona Western College. He has served in the United States Armed Forces (Branch of the Air Force) from 1983-88. He considers himself a tent maker like the apostle Paul by working as a school bus driver for one of the school districts in California.

On September 1986 he married the former Debra Ochoa in Anchorage, Alaska and has one daughter, Melissa. He and his family presently reside in Fresno, California.

He can be reach by e-mail dcruz77@sbcglobal.net

CPSIA information can be obtained at www.ICGtesting.com
Printed in the USA
BVOW04s2022120514

353306BV00005B/116/P

9 781629 523736